HTML

Basic Fundamental Guide for Beginners

TABLE OF CONTENTS

Introduction

Congratulations and thank you for purchasing *HTML: Basic Fundamental Guide For Beginners*! Whether you're interested in learning HTML to build your own basic website or you'd just like to expand your understanding of markup languages, this book is a great starting point and will provide you with easy-to-understand explanations and examples. In no time you'll be able to use your newly learned HTML skills to create a simple yet functional website.

Never used a programming or markup language before? Don't panic! You don't need much to begin—in fact, all you need to get started with learning HTML is a simple program for editing text (like Notepad or TextEdit) and a web browser to view your creations. In the following chapters, you'll learn not only what HTML is and what it can be used for but also gain an understanding of basic HTML through descriptions and samples that you can easily reproduce yourself. Excited about designing your very own website? By the time you complete this book, you will be able to apply what you've learned to create a simple page with different fonts, eye-catching colors, a unique layout, tables, lists, and even a form that will accept input from a user!

There are many books available on this subject, so thanks again for choosing this one. Good luck and have fun getting started with HTML!

Chapter 1

Getting Started With Basic HTML Tags

Before getting started with writing your first small chunk of HTML, it's necessary that you understand what HTML is. Literally, HTML is an initialism for HyperText Markup Language, which is a set of codes and symbols used to mark up a file so that a web browser knows how to display the content of the file. *Without* HTML, a browser would just display your web page as plain text without any sorts of fonts, colors, or layout; *with* HTML, a browser knows how to display your web page in exactly the style and format that you want. Generally speaking, HTML defines the way that a web page—and the internet as a whole—will appear to users.

In order to give a browser instructions about how to display a file, HTML uses something called tags to signify the beginnings and ends of elements. These tags contain information called attributes which allow a browser to know how the element should appear. The next few sections discuss how elements, tags, and attributes work to define how your web page content will look.

What are elements, tags, and attributes?

In HTML, an element is a single component of your web page. Generally, each element on your page will have both a start and end tag as well as some sort of content, though certain "empty elements" only require a start tag. Both kinds of tags are labels enclosed in the <> symbols that a browser uses to know how to display a page, but the tags themselves are not displayed. Tags are commonly written in lowercase despite the fact that HTML is not case sensitive. Take a look at the format of an HTML element:

A little bit of content

You can see that the element begins with a tag called "sometagname" which is enclosed in the <> symbols. At the end of the content, you can see the end tag. You'll notice that the end tag is almost identical to the start tag with the addition of the / symbol before the tag name inside the <> symbols. Some elements will display accurately even if the end tag is missing, but sometimes a missing end tag will create an error, so it's best to ensure that your end tags are always in place.

The start tag for an element can define attributes for the element which can give the browser a little bit more information about how the element should be displayed. For instance, an attribute of a link element could be the URL destination for the link. Attributes of an image might include its display height and width. For text, attributes could be styling information like what color, size, or font it should be displayed as. An element can have multiple attributes, so you can fully customize the components of your web pages.

Attributes are contained within the start tag after the tag name and consist of the attribute name followed by the = symbol and then the attribute information in quotation marks. The basic format should look like this:

<sometagname someattributename="attribute value">

A little bit of content

</sometagname>

Similar to the tag name, the attribute name should be written in lowercase. The attribute value should be contained in either single or double quotations. It is worth noting here that if your attribute value itself contains single or double quotation marks, you will need to use the opposite to enclose the attribute value. For instance, if your attribute value is the phrase "You're awesome!" you'll need to enclose it with double quotes, like so:

    someattributename="You're awesome!"

Alternatively, if your attribute value is something like "Amanda "Mandy" Jones," then you should enclose it with single quotes:

    someattributename='Amanda "Mandy" Jones'

If this seems a little overwhelming, don't worry! Over the course of the next couple of sections, you'll have the opportunity to view some actual examples of working HTML and you'll have the opportunity to gain some hands-on experience.

How do I get started with my first web page?

Now that you have a basic idea of how HTML uses tags to tell a browser how to display content, it's time to put that knowledge to use! Throughout this next section, you'll learn some ways that you can use HTML to put together a very basic web page. Open up Notepad, TextEdit, or your favorite text editor and follow along.

Note: if you're a Mac user using TextEdit, you may need to adjust some settings in order to view and save things properly. Under Preferences and then Format, you'll want to select "Plain Text," and under Open and Save, you'll need to check a box that says "Display HTML files as HTML code instead of formatted text."

The very first thing you'll need to include whenever you start writing an HTML document is the following line:

<!DOCTYPE html>

This line is not an element even though it uses the <> symbols just like element tags do. This line is a declaration, and it lets the browser know that the document is written using HTML. If this line is not present, the browser may attempt to display the web page using some default styles, but certain elements may not show up correctly. It's important to always include this line.

The next component of your HTML file will be the root element of your page, and it will surround the remainder of the HTML in your file. This root element will have <html> start and end tags, so your HTML document so far will look like this:

<!DOCTYPE html>
<html>

</html>

You'll notice that there's some space between the <html> start and end tags—that's where the rest of your elements will be written. HTML allows elements to be nested, which means an element can actually contain another element or even multiple elements. The first element that will be contained inside of the <html> root element will be the <head> element, which contains metadata or data about the HTML document. This metadata can define information like the title of a document, scripts, links to CSS stylesheets, descriptions of your web page, and styles. For this first example, we'll just be putting the title of the document you're wanting to create into the <head> element, so the HTML document will look similar to this:

```
<!DOCTYPE html>
<html>
<head>
<title> Just an Example Web Page </title>
</head>
</html>
```

The text that is contained inside of the <title> element—in this example, Just an Example Web Page—is what will show up in a browser tab as the name of the page. It's also what the page will be called if you add it to your favorites or find it somewhere online, such as in results from a search engine.

You may notice that in our sample, the <head> element start and end tags are indented under the root <html> element, and after that the <title> element is indented within the <head> element. This is not necessary, but it can help when writing your HTML document to see how elements are laid out. The page will display the same whether or not the element tags are indented, however, so it's up to you to write your HTML documents in whichever way you feel the most comfortable.

Of course, you won't just want your web page to be a blank page with a title, so you'll need to have a space to put all of the content you want to be displayed on your page. You'll do this within another element within the <html> element called the <body> element. It will come after the <head> element like so:

```
<!DOCTYPE html>
<html>
<head>
<title> Just an Example Webpage </title>
</head>
<body>

</body>
</html>
```

The <body> element of your HTML document will contain everything that is visible on your web page like text, pictures, links, and media. For this simple example, we'll just be adding a couple lines of text to your page: one large heading and one smaller paragraph. Now, your HTML document will look like this:

```
<!DOCTYPE html>
<html>
<head>
<title> Just an Example Webpage </title>
</head>
<body>
    <h1> Example of headings in HTML. </h1>
    <p> Example of paragraphs in HTML. </p>
    <p> Second example of paragraphs in HTML </p>
</body>
</html>
```

The heading element starts with the <h1> tag and ends with the </h1> tag, and the paragraph elements start and end with the <p> and </p> tags. You can see that the heading and the paragraph elements are separate from each other but are all contained within the <body> element. Make sure to use end tags, and be sure to put them in the appropriate places.

That's it! You now have a simple HTML document that will display a simple web page in a browser. In order to test it out, you'll first need to save your HTML document with the correct file extension. Click "Save as" in the menu, and then put the file name **myexamplewebpage.html** in the "File name" box. Don't forget the .html extension! Next, change the "Save as type" to "All Files (*.*)" and click Save. Now you can open your HTML file in your browser window either by double-clicking on it from where you saved it or by clicking the file with your right mouse button and picking "Open with." When your page opens, it should look something like this:

This line is a heading.

This line is a paragraph.

This line is also a paragraph.

In the URL bar, you should be able to see the file path to the HTML document you created; it will probably look similar to this, but not exactly the same. You can see from this example how the page title, heading, and paragraphs are displayed. The browser utilizes the HTML tags to decide how to show the text content, but the tags themselves are not shown.

How can I change the appearance of the elements on my web page?

Now that you have a basic framework for your HTML pages, you'll undoubtedly want to start adding custom elements to create a page that fits your personal needs. Check out some of the different tags below that you can use to completely customize your sites:

<title> </title>

The <title> element contains the name of your web page, which is displayed in a browser tab or within search engine results. Be sure to title your page something informative!

\<style> \</style>

These tags contain information about the default styles your document will use and are located inside the \<head> element of your HTML document. Alternatively, one can set the style for an individual element within its start tag.

\<meta>

This tag and its attributes define information about your web page, like a page description, page author, or keywords relevant to your page. This tag is contained in the \<head> element and does not show anything on your page itself.

\<script> \</script>

These tags contain JavaScript code that can be used elsewhere on your page to perform actions like manipulating images or validating forms.

\<p> \</p>

These tags signify the beginning and end of a paragraph. You used these in the example in the previous section. A paragraph is simply text that is spaced apart from surrounding elements.

\<b> \</b>

These tags signify that the contained text should be bold.

\<u> \</u>

These tags signify that the contained text should be underlined.

\<i> \</i>

These tags signify that the contained text should be italicized.

\<del> \</del>

These tags signify that the contained text was deleted and the text is displayed with a line through it.

\<mark> \</mark>

These tags signify that the contained text should be highlighted.

\<h1> \</h1>

These tags are used to display a large or very important heading.

\<h2> \</h2>

These tags are used to display a heading that is large and important, but less so than h1.

\<h3> \</h3>

These tags are used to display smaller or less important heading than h2.

\<h4> \</h4>

These tags are used to display smaller or less important heading than h3.

\<h5> \</h5>

These tags are used to display smaller or less important heading than h4.

\<h6> \</h6>

These tags are used to display the smallest-sized or least important heading.

<a> </a>

These tags are used to define a link. You'll use the href attribute to specify the destination for the link and the link will be displayed as the text that is placed between the two given tags.

<img>

This tag is used to define an image and does not use an end tag. You can use attributes to control the source file for the image, the image size, and any alternative text for the image.

<button> </button>

These tags signify a button that can be clicked. You can use buttons along with JavaScript to perform certain actions when the buttons are clicked.

This tag signifies a line break and doesn't require an end tag. A line break is simply an empty line. You can use one or multiple line breaks between the elements on your page to space them out and prevent your layout from appearing jumbled.

HTML also uses certain element tags to help define the layout of your web page, such as the following:

<header> </header>

This element defines a section or document header.

<nav> </nav>

This element contains the navigation links for a web page.

\<section\> \</section\>

This element determines a section within a document.

\<aside\> \</aside\>

This element contains additional sidebar content on a web page.

\<footer\> \</footer\>

This element defines a section or document footer.

\<details\> \</details\>

This element contains additional details about the page.

You'll also want to familiarize yourself with the attributes that can be used with each of these tags. Some of the most common and important ones are as follows:

href

This attribute defines the URL for a link element. You'll want to use the full URL, including the http:// at the beginning.

src

This attribute signifies where the source file for an image can be found. This can be a file path or a URL. If the file in question and the HTML document are both saved in the same folder, you can simply use the filename and extension here; otherwise, you should use an absolute file path.

title

This attribute gives additional information about an element which is displayed when a cursor hovers over it. This can help users understand how to use certain aspects of your web page.

alt

This attribute provides alt text for an image which is displayed when the image itself can't be shown.

id

This attribute assigns a unique id to an element. Each id should only be used once per web page; an id is often used as a unique identifier for a particular element.

disabled

This attribute signifies that an element should be displayed as disabled on your web page. Disabled elements are usually greyed out, which prevents users from interacting with them.

height

This attribute defines how tall an element should be on your web page. It can be a set amount of pixels or even a percentage value.

width

This attribute defines how wide an element should be on your web page. It can be a set amount of pixels or even a percentage value.

style

This attribute can be used to define how an element is styled in terms of size, color, or font.

There are many other tags and attributes available for you to use, but they won't all be necessary for every web page you build, and certain elements can tend to be complex to use. For this beginner's tutorial, we'll be sticking to some of the simpler elements to create your page. Open up your text editor again and follow along!

For this example, we'll start off in the same way that we did with the first example, by beginning the document with the HTML declaration and the <html> start tag:

```
<!DOCTYPE html>
<html>
```

Then, we'll add some information into the <head> element, so put the <head> start tag on the next line:

```
<!DOCTYPE html>
<html>
    <head>
```

On the next line, we'll define the title of our web page, just like we did in our first sample:

```
<!DOCTYPE html>
<html>
    <head>
    <title> Another web page! </title>
```

Now we can add in something different. By using the <style> element, we can set default style information for our web page. Let's make it so that our web page has a blue background, white headings, and red paragraphs with a white background:

```
<!DOCTYPE html>
<html>
  <head>
  <title> Another web page! </title>

  <style>
      body {background-color: blue;}
      h1 {color: white;}
      p {color: red; background-color: white;}
</style>
```

Next, let's use the <meta> element to add some information about our web page to our document, like an author, a description, and some keywords for search engines to use:

```
<!DOCTYPE html>
<html>
  <head>
      <title> Another web page! </title>
      <style>
          body {background-color: blue;}
          h1 {color: white;}
          p {color: red; background-color: white;}
      </style>
      <meta name="author" content="Your Name">
      <meta name="description" content ="A basic web page sample">
      <meta name="keywords" content="HTML, sample, beginner">
```

Great! If you want to define any JavaScript functions or link to a CSS stylesheet you would also do that here in the <head> element, but for now, let's end the <head> element and put some customized elements into the <body> element:

```
<!DOCTYPE html>
<html>
  <head>
      <title> Another web page! </title>
      <style>
          body {background-color: blue;}
          h1 {color: white;}
          p {color: red; background-color: white;}
       </style>
       <meta name="author" content="Your Name">
       <meta name="description" content ="A basic web page sample">
       <meta name="keywords" content="HTML, sample, beginner">
  </head>
  <body>
```

First, let's add in a few different headings. Remember in the <head> element that you set the default color for <h1> elements to white. Let's add an <h1> element without any attributes, an <h1> element with a specified color attribute, and some other heading elements with various attributes to see how their sizes and styles compare:

```
<!DOCTYPE html>
<html>
  <head>
      <title> Another web page! </title>
      <style>
          body {background-color: blue;}
          h1 {color: white;}
          p {color: red; background-color: white;}
      </style>
      <meta name="author" content="Your Name">
      <meta name="description" content ="A basic web page
      sample">
      <meta name="keywords" content="HTML, sample,
      beginner">
  </head>
  <body>
      <h1> This is a heading using the defined default style.
      </h1>
      <h1 style="color:aqua;"> Example of headings being given
      defined color attributes. </h1>
      <h2 style="text-align:center;"> Example of centering
      subheadings using CSS properties. </h2>
      <h3 > This is a smaller subheading with the default style.
      </h3>
      <h4 style="background-color:black; color:white;"> This is
      an even smaller subheading with a defined color and
      background color. </h4>
      <h5 style="text-align:right;"> This is an even smaller
      subheading, and it's right justified! </h5>
      <h6 style="background-color:green;"> This is the smallest
      heading with a defined background color. </h6>
```

Now, let's add some text and some line breaks below your headings. Remember, one is able to nest elements within other ones!

```html
<!DOCTYPE html>
<html>
    <head>
        <title> Another web page! </title>
        <style>
            body {background-color: blue;}
            h1 {color: white;}
            p {color: red; background-color: white;}
        </style>
        <meta name="author" content="Your Name">
        <meta name="description" content ="A basic web page sample">
        <meta name="keywords" content="HTML, sample, beginner">
    </head>
    <body>
        <h1> This is a heading using the defined default style. </h1>
        <h1 style="color:aqua;"> Example of headings being given defined color attributes </h1>
        <h2 style="text-align:center;"> Example of centering subheadings using CSS properties. </h2>
        <h3 > This is a smaller subheading with the default style. </h3>
        <h4 style="background-color:black; color:white;"> This is an even smaller subheading with a defined color and background color. </h4>
        <h5 style="text-align:right;"> This is an even smaller subheading, and it's right justified! </h5>
        <h6 style="background-color:green;"> This is the smallest heading with a defined background color. </h6>
```

<p> Example of paragraphs using default style definition. </p>

<p style="background-color:blue; color:black;"> Example of the background color removed and a text color defined. </p>

<p style="font-size:200%;"> Example of doubling font size in paragraph. </p>

<p style="color:black;"> Example of <b> bold </b> , <i> italicized </i> , <u> underlined </u> , and <mark> highlighted </mark> words. </p>

<p> This is an example of <br> breaking up lines in HTML. </p>

<p style="font-family:courier; background-color:black; color:white;"> Example of a different font and a defined background color and text color. </p>

<p title="Hello!"> This paragraph shows some text when you hover over it. </p>

Next, let's put a link on our page that sends the user to the Google homepage when they click it:

```
<!DOCTYPE html>
<html>
    <head>
        <title> Another web page! </title>
        <style>
            body {background-color: blue;}
            h1 {color: white;}
            p {color: red; background-color: white;}
        </style>
        <meta name="author" content="Your Name">
        <meta name="description" content ="A basic web page
        sample">
        <meta name="keywords" content="HTML, sample,
        beginner">
    </head>
    <body>
        <h1> This is a heading using the defined default style.
        </h1>
        <h1 style="color:aqua;"> Example of headings being given
        defined color attributes </h1>
        <h2 style="text-align:center;"> Example of centering
        subheadings using CSS properties. </h2>
        <h3 > This is a smaller subheading with the default style.
        </h3>
        <h4 style="background-color:black; color:white;"> This is
        an even smaller subheading with a defined color and
        background color. </h4>
        <h5 style="text-align:right;"> This is an even smaller
        subheading, and it's right justified! </h5>
        <h6 style="background-color:green;"> This is the smallest
        heading with a defined background color. </h6>

        <p> Example of paragraphs using default style definition.
        </p>
```

```
<p style="background-color:blue; color:black;"> Example
of the background color removed and a text color defined.
</p>
<p style="font-size:200%;"> Example of doubling font size
in paragraph. </p>
<p style="color:black;"> Example of <b> bold </b> , <i>
italicized </i> , <u> underlined </u> , and <mark>
highlighted </mark> words. </p>
<p> This is an example of <br> breaking up lines in
HTML. </p>
<p style="font-family:courier; background-color:black;
color:white;"> Example of a different font and a defined
background color and text color. </p>
<p title="Hello!"> This paragraph shows some text when
you hover over it. </p>

<a style="color:white;" href="http://www.google.com">
Outgoing anchor to Google </a>
```

Finally, let's put a picture onto your web page. You can use an image that you have saved on your computer or you can use one online. To use an image from your own computer, you'll need to save the image in the same location as your HTML document. For instance, if your HTML document is saved on your desktop, your image should also be saved on your desktop; if your HTML document is saved in a folder, your image should be saved in the same folder. Let's add an image that's saved as shapes.png:

```html
<!DOCTYPE html>
<html>
    <head>
        <title> Another web page! </title>
        <style>
            body {background-color: blue;}
            h1 {color: white;}
            p {color: red; background-color: white;}
        </style>
        <meta name="author" content="Your Name">
        <meta name="description" content ="A basic web page sample">
        <meta name="keywords" content="HTML, sample, beginner">
    </head>
    <body>
        <h1> This is a heading using the defined default style. </h1>
        <h1 style="color:aqua;"> Example of headings being given defined color attributes </h1>
        <h2 style="text-align:center;"> Example of centering subheadings using CSS properties. </h2>
        <h3 > This is a smaller subheading with the default style. </h3>
        <h4 style="background-color:black; color:white;"> This is an even smaller subheading with a defined color and background color. </h4>
        <h5 style="text-align:right;"> This is an even smaller subheading, and it's right justified! </h5>
        <h6 style="background-color:green;"> This is the smallest heading with a defined background color. </h6>
        <p> Example of paragraphs using default style definition. </p>
```

```html
<p style="background-color:blue; color:black;"> Example
of the background color removed and a text color defined.
</p>
<p style="font-size:200%;"> Example of doubling font size
in paragraph. </p>
<p style="color:black;"> Example of <b> bold </b> , <i>
italicized </i> , <u> underlined </u> , and <mark>
highlighted </mark> words. </p>
<p> This is an example of <br> breaking up lines in
HTML. </p>
<p style="font-family:courier; background-color:black;
color:white;"> Example of a different font and a defined
background color and text color. </p>
<p title="Hello!"> This paragraph shows some text when
you hover over it. </p>

<a style="color:white;" href="http://www.google.com">
Outgoing anchor to Google </a>

<img src="shapes.png">
```

If you'd like to change the size of the image, you can do so using the width and height attributes. You can also add some alternative text to the image using the alt attribute:

```html
<!DOCTYPE html>
<html>
    <head>
        <title> Another web page! </title>
        <style>
            body {background-color: blue;}
            h1 {color: white;}
            p {color: red; background-color: white;}
        </style>
        <meta name="author" content="Your Name">
        <meta name="description" content ="A basic web page sample">
        <meta name="keywords" content="HTML, sample, beginner">
    </head>
    <body>
        <h1> This is a heading using the defined default style. </h1>
        <h1 style="color:aqua;"> Example of headings being given defined color attributes </h1>
        <h2 style="text-align:center;"> Example of centering subheadings using CSS properties. </h2>
        <h3 > This is a smaller subheading with the default style. </h3>
        <h4 style="background-color:black; color:white;"> This is an even smaller subheading with a defined color and background color. </h4>
        <h5 style="text-align:right;"> This is an even smaller subheading, and it's right justified! </h5>
        <h6 style="background-color:green;"> This is the smallest heading with a defined background color. </h6>
        <p> Example of paragraphs using default style definition. </p>
```

\<p style="background-color:blue; color:black;"\> Example of the background color removed and a text color defined. \</p\>

\<p style="font-size:200%;"\> Example of doubling font size in paragraph. \</p\>

\<p style="color:black;"\> Example of \<b\> bold \</b\> , \<i\> italicized \</i\> , \<u\> underlined \</u\> , and \<mark\> highlighted \</mark\> words. \</p\>

\<p\> This is an example of \<br\> breaking up lines in HTML. \</p\>

\<p style="font-family:courier; background-color:black; color:white;"\> Example of a different font and a defined background color and text color. \</p\>

\<p title="Hello!"\> This paragraph shows some text when you hover over it. \</p\>

\<a style="color:white;" href="http://www.google.com"\> Outgoing anchor to Google \</a\>

\<img src="shapes.png"\>

\<img src="shapes.png" width="750" height="500" alt="A square, a circle, and a triangle."\>

Great! Now, close the \<body\> and \<html\> elements, and you should have an HTML document that looks like this:

```
<!DOCTYPE html>
<html>
    <head>
        <title> Another web page! </title>
        <style>
            body {background-color: blue;}
            h1 {color: white;}
            p {color: red; background-color: white;}
        </style>
        <meta name="author" content="Your Name">
        <meta name="description" content ="A basic web page
        sample">
        <meta name="keywords" content="HTML, sample,
        beginner">
    </head>
    <body>
        <h1> This is a heading using the defined default style.
        </h1>
        <h1 style="color:aqua;"> Example of headings being given
        defined color attributes </h1>
        <h2 style="text-align:center;"> Example of centering
        subheadings using CSS properties. </h2>
        <h3 > This is a smaller subheading with the default style.
        </h3>
        <h4 style="background-color:black; color:white;"> This is
        an even smaller subheading with a defined color and
        background color. </h4>
        <h5 style="text-align:right;"> This is an even smaller
        subheading, and it's right justified! </h5>
        <h6 style="background-color:green;"> This is the smallest
        heading with a defined background color. </h6>
        <p> Example of paragraphs using default style definition.
        </p>
```

```
<p style="background-color:blue; color:black;"> Example
of the background color removed and a text color defined.
</p>
<p style="font-size:200%;"> Example of doubling font size
in paragraph. </p>
<p style="color:black;"> Example of <b> bold </b> , <i>
italicized </i> , <u> underlined </u> , and <mark>
highlighted </mark> words. </p>
<p> This is an example of <br> breaking up lines in
HTML. </p>
<p style="font-family:courier; background-color:black;
color:white;"> Example of a different font and a defined
background color and text color. </p>
<p title="Hello!"> This paragraph shows some text when
you hover over it. </p>
<a style="color:white;" href="http://www.google.com">
Outgoing anchor to Google </a>
<br>
<br>
<img src="shapes.png">
<br>
<br>
<img src="shapes.png" width="750" height="500" alt="A
square, a circle, and a triangle.">
</body>
</html>
```

When you save this document with a .html extension and open it using
a browser, it will look something like this:

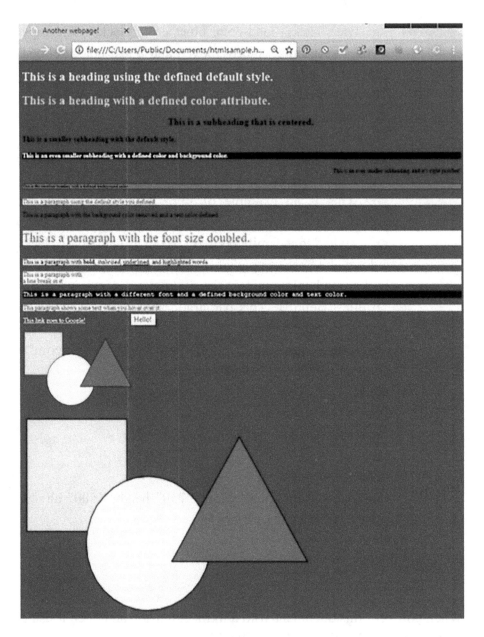

Congratulations! You've made an HTML page with customized elements. Feel free to play around with the tags and attributes for these sample elements to make a simple web page that suits your personal needs. Try to practice creating different custom elements, like an image that links to another website, or a heading that shows a message when you hover over it with a cursor.

Chapter 2

Creating HTML Lists And Tables

In addition to headings and paragraphs, you may want to display your text in other formats, such as a list or a table. Fortunately, HTML makes this simple to do using tags just like the ones you practiced using in the previous chapter. Follow along through the next sections to see additional ways you can format the content of your web page.

How can I display my content as a list?

If you'd like to display a portion of the content on your web page as a list, you actually have a couple of different options to do so. For lists in which you would like the items to have a defined order, you can create what is called an ordered list, which uses numbers, letters, or numerals next to the list items. Ordered lists are defined using the <ol> tag, and each item in the list uses a <li> tag. For instance, if you'd like to create a list of race participants by the order in which they finished, you might have something like this:

```
<ol>
   <li> Susan </li>
   <li> Mark </li>
   <li> Amanda </li>
   <li> Jon </li>
</ol>
```

which will number the participants from 1 to 4. You can use the **type** attribute to change the numbering system to upper or lowercase letters or upper or lowercase Roman numerals like so:

```
<ol type="1">
    <li> Susan </li>
    <li> Mark </li>
    <li> Amanda </li>
    <li> Jon </li>
</ol>

<ol type="A">
    <li> Susan </li>
    <li> Mark </li>
    <li> Amanda </li>
    <li> Jon </li>
</ol>

<ol type="a">
    <li> Susan </li>
    <li> Mark </li>
    <li> Amanda </li>
    <li> Jon </li>
</ol>

<ol type="I">
    <li> Susan </li>
    <li> Mark </li>
    <li> Amanda </li>
    <li> Jon </li>
</ol>

<ol type="i">
    <li> Susan </li>
    <li> Mark </li>
    <li> Amanda </li>
    <li> Jon </li>
</ol>
```

If you'd like, you also have the option to start numbering your ordered list from a specified point using the **start** attribute:

```
<ol start="10">
    <li> Brian </li>
    <li> David </li>
    <li> Lynn </li>
    <li> Sabrina </li>
</ol>

<ol start="50">
    <li> Louise </li>
    <li> Morgan </li>
    <li> Jana </li>
    <li> Peter </li>
</ol>
```

Alternatively, if the order of your list items doesn't matter, you can create an unordered list. Unordered lists use markers or bullets to mark individual list items, and are defined using the <ul> tag. Similarly to ordered lists, each individual list item is defined with the <li> tag, as follows:

```
<ul>
    <li> square </li>
    <li> triange </li>
    <li> rectangle </li>
    <li> circle </li>
</ul>
```

Unordered lists can also be customized using the **style** attribute. The default style is to use bullets, but you can also use squares, circles, or no markers at all to mark each item in your list, like so:

```
<ul style="list-style-type:square">
    <li> square </li>
    <li> triange </li>
    <li> rectangle </li>
    <li> circle </li>
</ul>

<ul style="list-style-type:circle">
    <li> square </li>
    <li> triange </li>
    <li> rectangle </li>
    <li> circle </li>
</ul>

<ul style="list-style-type:none">
    <li> square </li>
    <li> triange </li>
    <li> rectangle </li>
    <li> circle </li>
</ul>
```

You can further customize your lists by using the <b> , <i> , <u> , <a>, or <mark> tags around your text, just like you did with your paragraph text in the previous chapter. You can also nest lists within lists, like so:

```
<ul>
    <li> words </li>
        <ul>
            <li> normal </li>
            <li> <b> bold </b> </li>
            <li> <i> italicized </i> </li>
            <li> <mark> highlighted </mark> </li>
             <li> <a href="http://www.google.com"> link
            </a> </li>
        </ul>
```

```
<li> numbers </li>
    <ol>
        <li> one </li>
        <li> two </li>
        <li> three </li>
    </ol>
</ul>
```

Let's create another simple web page using headings and lists to see how different list types and styles appear in a browser. Type or copy and paste this next bit of HTML into your text editor:

```
<!DOCTYPE html>
<html>
    <head>
        <title> Lists! </title>
    </head>
    <body>
        <h3> An ordered list: </h3>
        <ol>
            <li> Susan </li>
            <li> Mark </li>
            <li> Amanda </li>
            <li> Jon </li>
        </ol>

        <h3> An ordered list using uppercase letters: </h3>
        <ol type="A">
            <li> Susan </li>
            <li> Mark </li>
            <li> Amanda </li>
            <li> Jon </li>
        </ol>
```

```html
<h3> An ordered list using lowercase letters: </h3>
<ol type="a">
        <li> Susan </li>
        <li> Mark </li>
        <li> Amanda </li>
        <li> Jon </li>
</ol>


<h3> An ordered list using uppercase roman
numerals: </h3>
<ol type="I">
        <li> Susan </li>
        <li> Mark </li>
        <li> Amanda </li>
        <li> Jon </li>
</ol>


<h3> An ordered list using lowercase roman
numerals: </h3>
<ol type="i">
        <li> Susan </li>
        <li> Mark </li>
        <li> Amanda </li>
        <li> Jon </li>
</ol>

<h3> An ordered list starting at 10: </h3>
<ol start="10">
        <li> Brian </li>
        <li> David </li>
        <li> Lynn </li>
        <li> Sabrina </li>
</ol>
```

```
<h3> An unordered list: </h3>
<ul>
        <li> square </li>
        <li> triange </li>
        <li> rectangle </li>
        <li> circle </li>
</ul>

<h3> An unordered list using square markers: </h3>
<ul style="list-style-type:square">
        <li> square </li>
        <li> triange </li>
        <li> rectangle </li>
        <li> circle </li>
</ul>

<h3> An unordered list using circle markers: </h3>
<ul style="list-style-type:circle">
        <li> square </li>
        <li> triange </li>
        <li> rectangle </li>
        <li> circle </li>
</ul>

<h3> An unordered list using no markers: </h3>
<ul style="list-style-type:none">
        <li> square </li>
        <li> triange </li>
        <li> rectangle </li>
        <li> circle </li>
</ul>
```

```
<h3> Nested lists: </h3>
<ul>
        <li> words </li>
            <ul>
                    <li> normal </li>
                    <li> <b> bold </b> </li>
                    <li> <i> italicized </i> </li>
                    <li>    <mark>    highlighted
                    </mark> </li>
                    <li>    <a    href="http://www.
                    google.com"> link </a> </li>
            </ul>
        <li> numbers </li>
            <ol>
                    <li> one </li>
                    <li> two </li>
                    <li> three </li>
            </ol>
        </ul>
    </body>
</html>
```

Now save the document with a .html extension and then open it up using a browser. Your web page should look something like this:

An ordered list:

1. Susan
2. Mark
3. Amanda
4. Jon

An ordered list using uppercase letters:

A. Susan
B. Mark
C. Amanda
D. Jon

An ordered list using lowercase letters:

a. Susan
b. Mark
c. Amanda
d. Jon

An ordered list using uppercase roman numerals:

I. Susan
II. Mark
III. Amanda
IV. Jon

An ordered list using lowercase roman numerals:

i. Susan
ii. Mark
iii. Amanda
iv. Jon

An ordered list starting at 10:

10. Brian
11. David
12. Lynn
13. Sabrina

An unordered list:

- square
- triange
- rectangle
- circle

An unordered list using square markers:

- square
- triange
- rectangle
- circle

An unordered list using circle markers:

o square
o triange
o rectangle
o circle

An unordered list using no markers:

square
triange
rectangle
circle

Nested lists:

- words
    o normal
    o **bold**
    o *italicized*
    o highlighted
    o link
- numbers
    1. one
    2. two
    3. three

How can I display my content as a table?

You may also occasionally want to display content as a table on your web page. You can accomplish this by using the <table> , <tr> , <th> and <td> tags. The <tr> tag signifies a row of the table, while the <th> and <td> tags specify table headers and table date respectively.

Consider a table with three columns that contain the first name, last name, and birthday for a set of individuals. Your HTML might look something like this:

```
<table>
    <tr>
            <th> First Name </th>
            <th> Last Name </th>
            <th> Birthday </th>
    </tr>
    <tr>
            <td> Rebecca </td>
            <td> Jones </td>
            <td> May 2 </td>
    </tr>
    <tr>
            <td> Tony </td>
            <td> White </td>
            <td> April 14 </td>
    </tr>
    <tr>
            <td> Jamie </td>
            <td> Parker </td>
            <td> August 27 </td>
    </tr>
</table>
```

You can use attributes to customize the size and text alignment of the elements in your table. For instance, you can alter the <table> element's **style** attribute to set your table to cover a set width or the whole width of your web page, and you can use the **text-align** attributes for the headers and cells to left align, center align, or right align your text. *Note: you can put the text-align attribute into the start tags of each of your cells, but if you're using the same formatting for an entire table, it will probably be easier to include this styling* *information within the document's **<head>** element, like you did in Chapter 1.*

Give it a try! Type the following HTML into your text editor:

```
<!DOCTYPE html>

    <html>
      <head>
            <title> Tables! </title>
            <style>
                  th {text-align:left;}
                  td {text-align:center;}
            </style>
      </head>
      <body>
            <h3> A table with 3 columns that spans 75% of the
            window width: </h3>
            <table style="width:75%">
                  <tr style="background-color:grey;">
                        <th> First Name </th>
                        <th> Last Name </th>
                        <th> Birthday </th>
                  </tr>
                  <tr style="color:green;">
                        <td> Rebecca </td>
                        <td> Jones </td>
                        <td> May 2 </td>
                  </tr>
                  <tr style="color:blue;">
                        <td> Tony </td>
                        <td> White </td>
                        <td> April 14 </td>
                  </tr>
                  <tr style="color:purple;">
                        <td> Jamie </td>
```

```
            <td> Parker </td>
            <td> August 27 </td>
        </tr>
    </table>
</body>
</html>
```

When you save it with the .html file extension and open it with your browser, it should look like this:

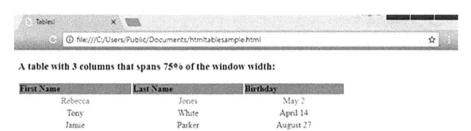

If you'd like, you can add borders to your table elements using the **border** attribute. You can instruct these separate borders to mesh into one border with the **border-collapse** attribute:

```
<style>
    table, th, td {border: 1px solid black; border-collapse:collapse;}
</style>
```

You can also use the colspan and rowspan attributes to create cells that cover multiple columns or rows. For instance, if two individuals had the same birthday in the above example, you might want to display it like so:

```
<tr>
    <th> First Name </th>
    <th> Last Name </th>
    <th> Birthday </th>
</tr>
<tr>
```

```
    <td> Rebecca </td>
    <td> Jones </td>
    <td rowspan="2"> May 2 </td>
</tr>
<tr>
    <td> Tony </td>
    <td> White </td>
</tr>
<tr>
    <td> Jamie </td>
    <td> Parker </td>
    <td> August 27 </td>
</tr>
```

Try it yourself! Copy and paste or manually type the following bit of HTML into your own text editor:

```
<!DOCTYPE html>
<html>
    <head>
            <title> Tables! </title>
            <style>
                    table, th, td {border: 1px solid black; border-collapse:collapse;}
                    th {text-align:left;}
                    td {text-align:center;}
            </style>
    </head>
    <body>
                    <h3> A table with 3 columns that uses the default width and colors: </h3>
            <table>
                    <tr>
                            <th> First Name </th>
```

```html
                    <th> Last Name </th>
                    <th> Birthday </th>
            </tr>
            <tr>
                    <td> Rebecca </td>
                    <td> Jones </td>
                    <td> May 2 </td>
            </tr>
            <tr>
                    <td> Tony </td>
                    <td> White </td>
                    <td> April 14 </td>
            </tr>
            <tr>
                    <td> Jamie </td>
                    <td> Parker </td>
                    <td> August 27 </td>
            </tr>
</table>

<h3> A table with 3 columns that spans 75% of the
window width and uses defined colors: </h3>
<table style="width:75%">
        <tr style="background-color:grey;">
                <th> First Name </th>
                <th> Last Name </th>
                <th> Birthday </th>
        </tr>
        <tr style="color:green;">
                <td> Rebecca </td>
                <td> Jones </td>
                <td> May 2 </td>
        </tr>
        <tr style="color:blue;">
                <td> Tony </td>
```

```
                <td> White </td>
                <td> April 14 </td>
        </tr>
        <tr style="color:purple;">
                <td> Jamie </td>
                <td> Parker </td>
                <td> August 27 </td>
        </tr>
</table>


<h3> A table with 3 columns that spans 75% of the
window width and uses merged rows: </h3>
<table style="width:75%">
        <tr>
                <th> First Name </th>
                <th> Last Name </th>
                <th> Birthday </th>
        </tr>
        <tr>
                <td> Rebecca </td>
                <td> Jones </td>
                <td rowspan="2"> May 2 </td>
        </tr>
        <tr>
                <td> Tony </td>
                <td> White </td>
        </tr>
        <tr>
                <td> Jamie </td>
                <td> Parker </td>
                <td> August 27 </td>
        </tr>
</table>
    </body>
</html>
```

Once you save this HTML with the .html extension and open it with a browser, your web page should look something like this:

A table with 3 columns that uses the default width and colors:

First Name	Last Name	Birthday
Rebecca	Jones	May 2
Tony	White	April 14
Jamie	Parker	August 27

A table with 3 columns that spans 75% of the window width and uses defined colors:

First Name	Last Name	Birthday
Rebecca	Jones	May 2
Tony	White	April 14
Jamie	Parker	August 27

A table with 3 columns that spans 75% of the window width and uses merged rows:

First Name	Last Name	Birthday
Rebecca	Jones	May 2
Tony	White	
Jamie	Parker	August 27

What other ways can I display my content?

In addition to lists and tables, you can also use HTML to format your text into block quotations, subscripts, superscripts, computer code, and even reversed text. Check out the following HTML to see how to use tags to format your page using these different techniques:

```
<!DOCTYPE html>
<html>
   <head>
          <title> Other Formats! </title>
   </head>
   <body>
          <h3> The following is a block quotation: </h3>
          <blockquote> This is a block quotation. Usually,
          browsers indent block quotations. You can use this tag
          when you want to quote long pieces of text from other
          sources. </blockquote>
          <h3> The following text contains subscript and
          superscript: </h3>
          <p> This paragraph uses <sub> subscript </sub> and
          <sup> superscript </sup> elements, which can be
          useful when working with math. </p>
          <h3> The following text is formatted to look like
          computer code: </h3>
          <code> If your page is relevant to programming, you
          might want to use this tag. </code>
          <h3> The following text is displayed right to left:
          </h3>
          <bdo dir="rtl"> Right to left! </bdo>
   </body>
</html>
```

Save the code prior in an HTML file and then open the file in your browser, and it should display like so:

The following is a block quotation:

> This is a block quotation. Usually, browsers indent block quotations. You can use this tag when you want to quote long pieces of text from other sources.

The following text contains subscript and superscript:

This paragraph uses $_{subscript}$ and ^{superscript} elements, which can be useful when working with math.

The following text is formatted to look like computer code:

`If your page is relevant to programming, you might want to use this tag.`

The following text is displayed right to left:

!tfel ot thgiR

Now that you've seen many of the different ways you can format and style the elements on your web page, try your hand at combining the techniques you've learned to further customize your page. Will you make a table with links? A page full of quotes? Interesting color coded informational tables? It's up to you!

Chapter 3

Creating HTML Forms And Handling Input

Oftentimes, when you are creating web pages, you are doing so with the intention of interacting with people who visit your page. One simple way to accomplish this is by incorporating an HTML form into your page to request input from your users.

What kinds of input can I accept from users?

Depending on the type of information you'd like to request from your users, you can incorporate a number of different input options into your forms. For instance, if you'd like a way for users to input their names, you could use a text input field. If you want users to choose from different available options, you could use radio buttons or a dropdown list of choices. Check out the options below for ways that you can use forms to request information from your users:

Text Fields: You can create a text field that is one line high through setting the input tag as **"text"** like so:

```
Type your first name here:
<br>
<input type="text"> </input>
```

Or, if you want to accept a larger quantity of text, like a message, you can create a text area using the <textarea> and </textarea> start and end tags.

Number Fields: You can create a field where users can input numerical values through setting the input tag as **"number"** like this:

> Please enter a number:
>
> <input type="number"> </input>

A number field will not allow the user to enter in any characters besides numbers.

Password Fields: You can create a field where users can enter their password by setting the input tag as **"password"** like so:

> Type your password here:
>
> <input type="password"> </input>

When a user types text into a password field, the characters are hidden for privacy.

Email Fields: You can create a field that accepts email addresses by setting the input tag as **"email"**, like this:

> Type your email address here:
>
> <input type="email"> </input>

This field will require a user to enter a text value containing the @ symbol.

Radio Buttons: You can set the input tag to **"radio"** to create radio buttons like so:

> <input type="radio" name="radiobuttons"> Option 1 </input>
> <input type="radio" name="radiobuttons"> Option 2 </input>
> <input type="radio" name="radiobuttons"> Option 3 </input>

Your user will only be able to select one of the available radio buttons at a time for radio buttons with the same **name** attribute value.

Checkboxes: You can create checkboxes for your forms by setting the input tag as **"checkbox"** as follows:

```
<input type="checkbox"> I like coffee </input>
<input type="checkbox"> I like tea </input>
```

Using checkboxes will let you users select none, some, or all of the options provided.

Drop-Down Lists: If you'd like to create a drop-down list with options for a user to choose from, you can do so by using the <select> and <option> tags like this:

```
<select>
    <option> Square </option>
    <option> Circle </option>
    <option> Triangle </option>
    <option> Hexagon </option>
</select>
```

Depending on the attributes you use, your user will be able to select either a single or multiple options from the drop-down list at a time.

Buttons: You can create a button that users can click on by setting the input tag to **"button"**. You can assign text to the button using the **value** attribute like so:

```
<input type="button" value="I'm a button!"> </input>
```

Note: nothing will happen when you click this button as is; you will need to assign it an action when it is clicked using the **onclick** attribute, which you'll see in the next section.

Color Choosers: You can allow your users to select a color using a color picker by setting the input tag to **"color"** like this:

```
Please choose your favorite color:
<br>
<input type="color"> </input>
```

Date Selectors: You can allow your users to select a date from a calendar by setting the input tag to **"date"** like this:

> Please select your birthdate:
>
> <input type="date"> </input>

Range Sliders: Your users can select a relative value on a sliding scale with a range slider which you can create by setting the input tag to **"range"** like so:

> Cold
> <input type="range"> </input>
> Hot

Submit Buttons: The submit button sends the data from your form to a handler, which processes the data from the form. You can create a submit button by setting the input tag to **"submit"** like this:

> <input type="submit"> </input>

The submit button refers to the **action** attribute in the <form> start tag to know where to send the data, which is generally a page with a data processing script.

Reset Buttons: If you would like your users to be able to set all of the options in your form back to their original default values, you can incorporate a reset button by setting the input tag to **"reset"** like so:

> <input type="reset"> </input>

Each form you create will use the <form> and </form> start and end tags to specify where the form begins and ends. This allows certain elements to know what to send when the form is submitted and enables you to have multiple forms on one page which can be submitted individually. Copy and paste or manually type in the following HTML into your text editor to see how different basic form elements appear in by default:

51

```html
<!DOCTYPE html>
<html>
    <head>
            <title> Forms! </title>
    </head>
    <body>
            <h2> A form with multiple input types: </h2>
            <form>
                    <h3> A text field: </h3>
                    Type your name below:
                    <br>
                    <input type="text"> </input>

                    <h3> A number field: </h3>
                    Please enter your favorite number:
                    <br>
                    <input type="number"> </input>

                    <h3> A password field: </h3>
                    Type your password below:
                    <br>
                    <input type="password"> </input>

                    <h3> An email field: </h3>
                    Type your email below:
                    <br>
                    <input type="email"> </input>

                    <h3> Radio buttons: </h3>
                    <input    type="radio"    name="radiobuttons">
                    Option 1 </input>
                    <input    type="radio"    name="radiobuttons">
                    Option 2 </input>
                    <input    type="radio"    name="radiobuttons">
                    Option 3 </input>
```

```
<h3> Checkboxes: </h3>
<input type="checkbox"> I like coffee </input>
<input type="checkbox"> I like tea </input>

<h3> A drop-down list: </h3>
<select>
        <option> Square </option>
        <option> Circle </option>
        <option> Triangle </option>
        <option> Hexagon </option>
</select>

<h3> A color picker: </h3>
Please choose your favorite color:
<br>
<input type="color"> </input>

<h3> A date picker: </h3>
Please select your birthdate:
<br>
<input type="date"> </input>

<h3> A slider: </h3>
Cold
<input type="range"> </input>
Hot

<h3> Standard, submit, and reset buttons: </h3>
<input type="button" value="I'm a button!">
</input>
<input type="submit"> </input>
<input type="reset"> </input>
        </form>
    </body>
</html>
```

When you save this HTML in a file using the .html extension and then open it with a browser, your page should look something like this:

A form with multiple input types:

A text field:

Please enter your name:

A number field:

Please enter your favorite number:

A password field:

Please enter your password:

An email field:

Please enter your email address:

Radio buttons:

○ Option 1 ○ Option 2 ○ Option 3

Checkboxes:

☐ I like coffee ☐ I like tea

A drop-down list:

Square ▼

A color picker:

Please choose your favorite color:

A date picker:

Please select your birthdate:
mm/dd/yyyy

A slider:

Cold ———◻——— Hot

Standard, submit, and reset buttons:

I'm a button! Submit Reset

How can I customize the forms on my web page?

Just like you can use attributes to change certain aspects of the text and images on your page, you can use attributes to enhance the elements in your forms. Some of the most common attributes you might use when creating forms are the following:

name: You should use the **name** attribute to assign a reference name to elements or groups of elements. This will enable other elements to interact with the element and form handlers to know what each piece of input data should refer to. Certain elements need to have a **name** attribute value assigned in order to work correctly like the radio buttons in the last section. You should use descriptive values to define this attribute.

value: The **value** attribute allows you to assign default values to the elements in your forms. For instance, you could have a word or phrase populate in a text field when your form is generated, or you could have a radio button pre-selected.

required: This attribute signifies that the field is required and that the form cannot be submitted without a value entered.

disabled: This attribute signifies that the current field should be disabled and unable to accept any input from a user.

max: The value for this attribute will define the maximum value that the input field is able to accept.

maxlength: Similarly to the **max** attribute, the value of the **maxlength** attribute defines how many characters an input field is able to accept from the user.

min: The value for this attribute will define the minimum value that the input field is able to accept.

size: The value assigned to the **size** attribute defines how many characters wide an input field should be.

Other attributes only pertain to specific input types. Read through the HTML below to view some examples of attributes used for form elements:

```
<!DOCTYPE html>
<html>
   <head>
           <title> Forms! </title>
   </head>
   <body>
           <h2> A form with multiple input types: </h2>
           <form>
                   <h3> A text field with a specified size, a default
value, and a maximum input length: </h3>
                   Please enter your first name:
                   <br>
                   <input       type="text"       value="Mario"
maxlength="10" size="12" name="firstname"> </input>


                   <h3> A disabled text field: </h3>
                   Please enter your last name:
                   <br>
                   <input type="text" name="lastname" disabled>
</input>


                   <h3> A large text area: </h3>
                   Please write a message:
                   <br>
                   <textarea       rows="5"       cols="35"
name="msgbox"> Some default text! </textarea>


                   <h3> A number field with a maximum accepted
value of 10: </h3>
                   Please enter your favorite number less than or
equal to 10:
```


<input   type="number"   max="10" name="favnum"> </input>

A number field with a specified step value: </h3>
Please enter a multiple of 5:

<input   type="number"   step="5" name="favnum"> </input>

A long password field: </h3>
Please enter your password:

<input   type="password"   name="password" size="60"> </input>

An email field that requires input: </h3>
Please enter your email address:

<input type="email" name="email" required> </input>

Radio buttons with one checked by default: </h3>
<input   type="radio"   name="textstyle">   <b> bold </b> </input>
<input type="radio" name="textstyle" checked> <i> italics </i> </input>
<input type="radio" name="textstyle"> <mark> highlighted </mark> </input>

Checkboxes that are checked by default: </h3>

```html
                <input    type="checkbox"    name="beverages"
checked> I like coffee </input>
                <input    type="checkbox"    name="beverages"
checked> I like tea </input>


                <h3> A drop-down list that allows users to pick
one option, with one selected by default: </h3>
                <select name="ashape">
                        <option> Square </option>
                        <option> Circle </option>
                        <option selected> Triangle </option>
                        <option> Hexagon </option>
                </select>


                <h3> A drop-down list that shows 2 options at a
time and allows users to pick multiple options using the ctrl key:
</h3>
                <select name="shapes" size="2" multiple>
                        <option> Square </option>
                        <option> Circle </option>
                        <option> Triangle </option>
                        <option> Hexagon </option>
                </select>


                <h3> A color picker: </h3>
                Please choose your favorite color:
                <br>
                <input       type="color"       name="favcolor">
</input>


                <h3> A date picker with date restrictions: </h3>
                Please select a date in 2000:
                <br>
                <input       type="date"       name="somedate"
min="2000-01-01" max="2000-12-31"> </input>
```

```html
<h3> A slider set to the minimum value by default: </h3>
Cold
<input type="range" value="0"> </input>
Hot

<h3> Standard, submit, and reset buttons: </h3>
<input type="button" onclick="alert('You clicked me!')" value="I'm a button!"> </input>
<input type="submit" value="Submit form!"> </input>
<input type="reset" value="Reset form!"> </input>
</form>
</body>
</html>
```

Save this HTML with a .html extension and open it with your browser. It should look like this:

A form with multiple input types:

A text field with a specified size, a default value, and a maximum input length:

Please enter your first name:
Mario

A disabled text field:

Please enter your last name:

A large text area:

Please write a message:
Some default text!

A number field with a maximum accepted value of 10:

Please enter your favorite number less than or equal to 10:

A number field with a specified step value:

Please enter a multiple of 5:

A long password field:

Please enter your password:

An email field that requires input:

Please enter your email address:

Radio buttons with one checked by default:

○ **bold** ● *italics* ○ highlighted

Checkboxes that are checked by default:

☑ I like coffee ☑ I like tea

A drop-down list that allows users to pick one option, with one selected by default:

Triangle ▾

A drop-down list that shows 2 options at a time and allows users to pick multiple options using the ctrl key:

Square
Circle

A color picker:

Please choose your favorite color:

A date picker with date restrictions:

Please select a date in 2000:
mm/dd/2000

A slider set to the minimum value by default:

Cold ⬛─────────── Hot

Standard, submit, and reset buttons:

I'm a button! Submit form! Reset form!

60

Great job! Now, play around with the elements of your form. What happens if you try to enter a value of 11 into the number field with a maximum value of 10? What about if you try to type more than 10 characters into the first text field? See how you can manipulate the different elements of your HTML form in ways that can be useful for your web page!

Chapter 4

HTML And CSS

In previous examples, you learned how to define the style for your elements in 2 different ways: in the start tag for the element itself, or within the <style> element within the <head> element of your HTML file. In doing so, you were actually using CSS already using inline and internal techniques. Next, let's look at how to define styles for your page and its elements externally using a separate CSS file.

What is CSS?

The initials CSS literally stand for the words Cascading Style Sheets. With CSS, you can define the style for a specific element, a type of element, or for your entire webpage easily and efficiently. Although you can use CSS within your HTML document or even within an individual element, perhaps the most efficient way to use CSS is by defining the styles for your website within an external document saved with a .css extension. By doing so, you enable yourself to alter the appearance of your entire website by changing a single file instead of individual pages or elements.

An external style sheet cannot contain any HTML code. The contents of your external CSS file will resemble the contents of the <style> element within the <head> element of an HTML document. If you've been following along with the examples in the previous chapters, this should look familiar to you! A simple .css file might look like this:

```
body {
    background-color: black;
}
h2 {
    color: white;
}
p {
    background-color: white;
    color: blue;
    font-family: courier;
}
```

Type the CSS from above into your text editor and save it with a .css extension as something like styles.css. To use the .css file with an HTML document, you will first need to define a link to the .css file within the <head> element of your HTML. Let's use a simple HTML example:

```
<!DOCTYPE html>
<html>
    <head>
            <title> CSS! </title>
            <link rel="stylesheet" href="styles.css"> </link>
    </head>
    <body>
            <h2> This heading uses the styles defined in your
            external CSS file! </h2>
            <p> This paragraph uses the styles defined in your
            external CSS file! </p>
    </body>
</html>
```

Save this HTML with a .html file extension in the same folder as your styles.css file. When you open the .html file using your browser, you should be able to see a heading and paragraph displayed using the styles you defined in your CSS file:

How can CSS enhance my web page?

You've already used CSS throughout this tutorial to style the elements of your webpage. By using an external .css style sheet, you can make the process of styling your webpage even simpler by containing all of your style rules in one place. You can use your style sheet to define how different types of elements should each be displayed in terms of sizes, fonts, colors, outlines, margins, and alignment, and then link to the same .css file from multiple HTML documents. Even if your website has 100 pages, you'll only have to write your CSS once!

In addition to assigning styles to specific element types like headings and paragraphs, you can also assign unique styles to individual elements using CSS. Let's take a look at a couple of different ways we can do this. The first way uses the id attribute within the start tag of an element.

For instance, let's slightly alter the HTML and CSS examples from the last section:

```
<!DOCTYPE html>
<html>
   <head>
          <title> CSS! </title>
          <link rel="stylesheet" href="styles.css"> </link>
   </head>
   <body>
          <h2> This is a normal h2 heading </h2>
          <p> This is a normal paragraph </p>
          <p id="special"> Example of a special id </p>
   </body>
</html>
```

64

Now, update your styles.css file to the following:

```
body {
    background-color: black;
}
h2 {
    color: white;
}
p {
    background-color: white;
    color: blue;
    font-family: courier;
}
#special {
    color: green;
}
```

Upon opening your file with your web browser, you should be able to see that the element with the **"special"** id uses the style defined by **#special** in the .css file:

Note: no 2 elements should be given the same id within a single page, so this method should only be used to alter individual elements.

Alternatively, you can use classes to style subsets of element types with CSS. For example, you could divide your paragraphs into normal and special classes and then use CSS to assign a different color to the special paragraph class. Copy and paste or manually type the following CSS code within your editor of choice and save it as styles.css:

```
body {
    background-color: black;
}
h2 {
    color: white;
}
p {
    background-color: white;
    color: blue;
    font-family: courier;
}
p.special {
    background-color: grey;
    color: aqua;
}
```

Now copy and paste or manually type the following HTML into your text editor:

```
<!DOCTYPE html>
<html>
    <head>
        <title> CSS! </title>
        <link rel="stylesheet" href="styles.css"> </link>
    </head>
    <body>
        <h2> This is a heading </h2>
        <p> This is a normal paragraph </p>
        <p class="special"> Example of a special class </p>
    </body>
</html>
```

Once you save the HTML document and then open it with a browser, your page should resemble the following:

This is a heading

This is a normal paragraph

This is a paragraph with a special id

Since multiple elements can have the same class value, you can use this method to assign specific styles to large subsets of element types. Even better, you can update the style of all of the elements with the same class name by simply updating your .css file—there's no need to update each individual element inline!

To get an idea of how to further use an external style sheet to define how your HTML page is displayed, copy and paste or manually type the following CSS code within your editor of choice and save it as styles.css:

```
body {
    background-color: aqua;
    font-family: courier;
}
h1 {
}
h2 {
    color: purple;
    text-align: center;
}
h3 {
    color: green;
    font-family: verdana;
}
h4 {
    color: grey;
    font-family: times;
    text-align: right;
}
h5 {
    background-color: black;
```

67

```css
    color: white;
}
h6 {
    text-align: center;
}
h6.error {
    color: red;
    font-weight: bold;
}
p {
    background-color: white;
    color: blue;
    font-family: verdana;
}
p.fancy {
    background-color: grey;
    color: aqua;
    font-family: cursive;
}
p.important {
    font-weight: bold;
    font-size: 200%;
    text-transform: capitalize;
    text-align: center;
}
p.right {
    text-align: right;
}
#special {
    font-size: 300%;
    background-color: aqua;
    color: green;
}
img {
    background-color: black;
```

```
}
img.big {
    width: 100%;
    height: 100%;
}
img.bordered {
    border-color: white;
    border-width: medium;
    border-style: solid;
}
img.dashborder {
    border-width: medium;
    border-color: white;
    border-style: dashed;
}
```

Then, copy and paste or manually type the following HTML into your text editor:

```
<!DOCTYPE html>
<html>
    <head>
            <title> CSS! </title>
            <link rel="stylesheet" href="styles.css"> </link>
    </head>
    <body>
            <h1> This is an h1 heading </h1>
            <h2> This is an h2 heading </h2>
            <h3> This is an h3 heading </h3>
            <h4> This is an h4 heading </h4>
            <h5> This is an h5 heading </h5>
            <h6> This is an h6 heading </h6>
            <h6 class="error"> This is an h6 error heading </h6>
            <p> This is a paragraph </p>
            <p class="fancy"> This is a fancy paragraph </p>
```

```
            <p class="important"> This is an important paragraph
</p>
            <p class="right"> This is a right aligned paragraph
</p>
            <p id="special"> Example of a special id </p>
            <p class="fancy"> Another fancy paragraph! </p>
            <img src="shapes.png">
            <br>
            <img src="shapes.png" class="big">
            <br>
            <img src="shapes.png" class="bordered">
            <br>
            <img src="shapes.png" class="dashborder">
    </body>
</html>
```

Save both files in the same folder along with an image called shapes.png and then open the HTML document with your web browser. The elements of your page will be aligned, sized, colored, and bordered in the ways that you specified in your .css file!

Now that you've got a basic idea of how you are able to use external CSS files to specify different styles for the elements in your HTML documents, take some time to practice. The previous example used a .css file to define styles for headings, paragraphs, and images. See if you can apply the same techniques to style other elements like links, tables, lists, or form elements. You'll be efficiently making unique web pages with custom styles in no time!

Chapter 5

Using Div Elements

In HTML, and especially with the advent of HTML5, there are many different dividing elements one can use in order to break your document up into several different sections, all of which have their own specialty but function in similar ways.

Remember, HTML is ultimately a *markup* language. It's intended to take text and present it in a certain way using codified standards. This means that, to one extent or another, the language itself should ideally be easy to understand. In order to aid in making HTML easier to understand, certain conventions have been created that allow people to write better markup. Among these are these new divider elements.

The oldest divider element, and in fact one which has been around for quite a while, is the *div* element. The div element normally will take either an *ID* or a *class* (or both). These are defined in the markup for the div element.

We've already talked about both of these in passing but since IDs and classes are actually a concept that you're going to run into fairly often when you're working with HTML and CSS, it's worth taking a second to really start to understand what they are and what the difference is between them. They are different and you can absolutely use both in order to mark a single element.

IDs and classes are similar but functionally different in a fundamental way. IDs serve as a means for designating a single element. In this way, an ID is an identifier, hence the name "ID." You cannot have two elements with the same identifier. All identifiers must be unique.

Classes are parallel to identifiers. They allow you to designate a single *type* of element. So, if you wanted every element of your site that was designated as a *content-box* to have a drop shadow, you could do so by setting these to be of the class *content-box*.

Something may be designated through both an ID and a class. If you were to do this, then it would take the style properties from both (something we'll talk about more in-depth in the book specifically geared at CSS). If they both have a similar property, like border-color for instance, then the class definition will be superseded by the ID definition.

IDs and classes can be written in your markup like so:

```
<div id="idName" class="className">
    <!-- content -->
</div>
```

Note that you don't necessarily have to have both of these. You can have only one and that would be perfectly fine. You also don't have to have either of these. However, if you decide to use these, then that will give you a way to define further things for these markup elements both within your CSS and within any JavaScript or PHP code that you write. As a result, getting into the habit of using these is extremely important. You can use them with pretty much any element that you want to style, but there is a way to use them excessively and in places where they don't really belong, so only use them when they have a specific purpose within the context of your code.

Another divider element that you should know is the *nav* element. The nav element is intended to give you an easy way to mark out where the navigation bar in your code is. Like so:

```
<nav>
    <a href=""> Link 1 </a>
    <a href=""> Link 2 </a>
    <a href=""> Link 3 </a>
</nav>
```

One can also try the section element, which will allow one to break their code into sections. This is functionally similar to the *div* element, but the language is a bit clearer. Where div can be used for generally any division, the *section* element is particularly useful within the context of modern web design where one-page designs that are broken into singular sections in the code are the modus operandi.

While we're discussing dividing elements, it's also important that you understand how they work in the context of linking back to your site. You can actually use identifiers in order to link to a certain place on your page. For example, if you were to have a div called "endOfPage" by an ID, you could link to the page in a manner such that clicking the link would take you to the start of that division. Like so:

<a href="#endOfPage"> Go to the End of the Page. </a>

This is especially useful when you're linking within your own document and working with the aforementioned single-page designs.

You refer to identifiers with a pound sign and to classes using a period, just for the record.

Another important sectional divider that you should probably know is the *footer* element. This allows you to designate in clear language the *footer* of a given page. This works just like the nav, section, and div elements do.

With that, we've covered most of the major division elements that you're going to need to get started with HTML. You can style according to these division markers and then have a very expressive markup document that will clearly show what is what and where.

Conclusion

Thank you again for purchasing *HTML: Basic Fundamental Guide for Beginners*, and congratulations on making it to the end! Hopefully, you've gained some insight into how HTML uses tags, elements, and attributes to tell a browser how to display a web page, and had some fun designing your very own web page from scratch.

The next step is to let yourself get creative. Have an idea for a cool new web page? Try using your new HTML skills to bring it to life! As with any other skill, if you really want to continue progressing with HTML, the best way is to practice using it every chance you get—there are a ton of websites out there just waiting to be made, and that means a ton of opportunities for you.

Finally, if you found this book useful as you began on your HTML journey, please take a moment to review it on Amazon. Thank you, good luck, and enjoy your new website!

www.ingramcontent.com/pod-product-compliance
Lightning Source LLC
Chambersburg PA
CBHW070853070326
40690CB00009B/1821